The Orange Popsicle

*Six Influential Lessons that will
Inspire You to Change Your Life*

———————

Gary Gzik

Peter,

Success is a split second
decision – just make the
decision. Choose to enjoy life!
Enthusiastically,
Gary

The Orange Popsicle
Copyright © 2010 by BizXcel Inc.

ISBN 978-0-9864850-1-5

Printed in the USA.

Dedication

To my parents who shaped the man I am today: With unlimited support and encouragement you gave me the confidence to take risks and carve out an exciting and rewarding life. Words cannot express the depth of my love and gratitude.

To my wife Jane, and my children, Evan and Hannah: You sacrificed so that I could hone my craft. Your constant love and support is a true inspiration. You are the reason I do what I do. You are my heart and soul. I love you all so very much.

To my work family at BizXcel: We face each day with laughter and a determination to make a difference in people's lives. You have all contributed to this dream in your own special way. I am forever in your debt.

And last but not least, you the reader: It is your courage and conviction for personal growth and your conscious desire to build a better life that allows me to live out my own personal mission to motivate, inspire and empower people to live happier and more fulfilled lives.

Take pride while reading this book. A piece of you is in the words.

Contents

Introduction 3

1. Getting More Enjoyment Out of Life 8

2. Overcoming Your Fears 31

3. Finding Your Motivation 46

4. Discovering Your Life Purpose 59

5. Understanding the Role of Gratitude 75

6. Keeping a Positive Attitude 88

Conclusion 103

Preface

The Orange Popsicle: what does it mean? It's just a popsicle right? Ask a five year old and they'll tell you its happiness on a stick.

Do you remember hot summer days as a child when all you needed to break out in a grin was seeing that box of popsicles sitting out on the picnic table? All you needed to make your day was getting your hands on the orange one (or another favorite flavor). This book is about achieving that mindset again.

This is a subject very close to my heart. I have made it my life's work to help people learn how to enjoy more fulfilling lives. I wrote this book because I want to bring more happiness to others, to people like you. I want you to see the world again like a child – with no fear, open to all opportunities and possibilities.

Within these pages, you will learn how to shed the anxieties holding you back from better pursuits, gain the motivation necessary to achieve more success and develop the positive attitude to overcome any and all of life's challenges.

Living a life with no barriers isn't hard; you just need a little information and an open mind. Let me be your guide. Escape the regular, old routine you are trapped in and transform your life by bringing in more excitement and pleasure. Enjoy this book, perhaps with a popsicle.

What is Happiness?

Most folks are about as happy as they
make up their minds to be.

– Abraham Lincoln

Introduction

Happiness.

Happiness is what this book is about. Seems simple enough.

Not always. If I asked your friends and family if you were happy, what would they say to me? Probably yes, right?

However, appearances must be deceiving because you're reading this book, so ergo, you must be looking for more. It is all too easy to give the illusion of being happy without actually achieving it. Or you may be happy with parts of your life – you are happy with your family, you are happy with your health, you are happy with your career, your home, your hobbies, your investments and so on and so forth.

But <u>are</u> you happy? Just happy, plain and simple. Frequently, we mistake happiness <u>with</u> something for <u>being</u> happy.

"That would mean I'd have to be happy with everything about my life. Not possible," you say.

I'm here to tell you it is possible. And yes, you can achieve it.

When I was younger I always thought I knew what happiness was. I was always going out and doing things to make myself happy. More often than not, they didn't work, so I'd go out and try something different. I'd get bored, so I'd join a class. I'd feel empty, so I'd go buy something. But despite all this, I lacked a sense of satisfaction with my life, with myself. I felt like I was on a continuous treadmill searching for the next happiness fix. After a while I just found myself exhausted, but no happier. Do you feel this way? It's time to step off the treadmill.

What is Happiness?

Before we go any further, let's look at the definition of happiness itself. "Happiness" is a state of well-being characterized by emotions ranging from contentment to intense joy. Straightforward. Easy to understand. You've felt content while relaxing with a good book and a cup of coffee. At some point in your life, you've experienced intense joy – at your graduation, wedding or the birth of your child. So why are you not happy? Why is happiness continually eluding you?

For the past 24 years, I've been travelling the world working with people on personal development. Time after time people have asked me how they can bring more consistent happiness into their lives. And there's the key, consistency.

When was the last time that you were truly happy? Happy with every aspect of your life on a day-to-day basis. Think hard.

I'll bet it was when you were a child. As hard as it is for people to believe, we were born to be happy. Every person on this earth is meant to be happy. It's theirs and yours for the taking. As children, we are conditioned from the beginning to constantly be striving for happiness. If a child isn't happy, they let you know and continue to do so until the situation is rectified and they find their happiness again.

So how are children achieving consistent levels of happiness? There are several reasons:

1. Children are awestruck by the simplest parts of our world – things we've long ago taken for granted. Just watch a young child discover bubbles and you'll see.

2. Children have no fear, if they did, they'd never learn to stand, walk, run. Some have even tried to learn how to fly.

3. Children have imaginations and they constantly cultivate them. We've all watched a child play happily (there's that word again) for hours with a box while the expensive gift we knew they'd love goes ignored.

4. Children only see black and white, right and wrong. You can't argue the grey with a child.

5. Children speak their minds. They aren't afraid to tell it like it is. Anybody who has ever watched *Kids Say the Darndest Things* can attest to this point.

6. In a child's life, the most important part of the day is taking time to play. When was the last time that "play" made it to the top of your To Do List?

Besides these innate skills that drive children to find happiness and simply be happy, we teach children from an early age how to be happy.

Children's fables, fairy tales and story books do much more than entertain and delight little minds. They are instruction guides on how to be happy. As we get older, children's books are replaced by "adult" entertainment (get your mind out of the gutter, that's not what I'm talking about). Our downtime is filled with the evening news, usually bad (we've all heard the philosophy that "if it bleeds, it leads"), satirical sitcoms, cutthroat reality series that highlight the need for instant gratification in 40 days or less, whether that be finding your true love or a million dollars, and much more. Don't get me started on the likes of Jerry Springer and their effect on our happiness either! All of this is a long way from Max and his Wild Things.

When children are young, people are constantly telling them how to lead good lives. They are told over and over again about treating other people the way they would like to be treated, not judging a book by its cover, to always tell the truth. When a child says they can't do something, we are quick to tell them they can do anything. As we get older, there no longer seems to be that wise person there telling us how to live our lives. We are dependent on ourselves to make the right decisions and that doesn't always turn out the way we intended.

What happened then? How did you get to this point? Life, no doubt. You became tangled up in the distractions of trying to be a grown-up and along the way you forgot what true happiness is and how much you deserve it. I'm here to say, "No more!" No longer will you be forced to duck and bob what life throws at you and have to settle with being happy with only parts of your life. You will simply <u>be</u> happy.

This book will take you through the steps to leading a more fulfilling life that you can be proud of. Along the way we will gain insight on happiness from the masters – children. From their lessons you will learn how to take back what is rightfully yours.

Chapter 1: Getting More Enjoyment Out of Life

If I asked you how happiness worked, would you be able to tell me? No, it's not leprechauns and fairies. By not knowing how we become happy, many people are lost before they even start the journey.

Explaining Happiness

I like to explain happiness through the Happiness Quotient Continuum (HQC). This shows you how you reach happiness over time. Don't be mistaken in thinking becoming happy is a quick process. True happiness takes time and dedication. It's an active effort that involves changing all aspects of your lifestyle in order to achieve more fulfillment out of life. You need to set your sights on what makes you happy and then create the right frame of mind, practice the right habits daily and behave in a consistent way in order to set the foundation for a more enjoyable life.

We have to plan for our happiness. Often we put our happiness off as a "someday." You'll hear me use this term many times and I'm sure you've used it many times yourself, saying "Someday I'll do that." Or "Someday I'll go there." But as soon as you say it, you push it to the bottom of your priority list and it sits there gathering dust. You need to take an active approach. You need to start focusing on the right things, in the right way, at the right moment. Only this way can you finally get to your "someday." You need to map out your journey and take those steps.

Happiness Quotient Continuum

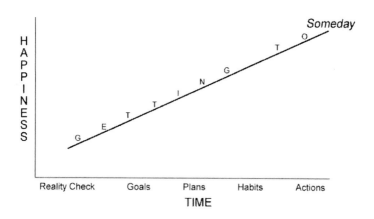

It is important to remember that the HQC takes in every aspect of your life: physical, emotional, mental and spiritual. If you are unhappy with one aspect of your life, then it isn't possible to achieve full happiness. This is again the difference between happiness <u>with</u> something and <u>being</u> happy.

Sidetracked

All of this seems simple enough, so why are so many people not happy? Often, on our path to "someday," we get sidetracked by gratification bounces. These disrupt our HQC. A gratification bounce is when we seek immediate gratification or a "happiness fix." We get our fix and we feel happy, for a while. These fixes are usually quick and easy, which makes them hard to pass by. We confuse them with true happiness instead of continuing to work towards our goals and building happiness over time. Often these fixes are based on decisions that do not support our HQC. We may do something immoral, unethical or even illegal because of the pull of happiness.

Gratification Bounces

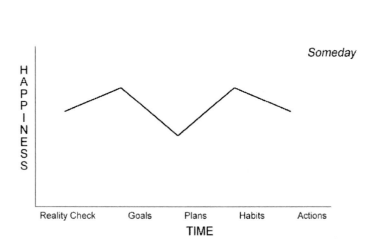

Instead of working steadily to reach our goals, we stray from the path in order to get a fix which then creates a spike in our graph. The problem with this spike is it is usually short lived and leads to the inevitable crash.

We've all been there, done that and bought the t-shirt. We start to feel a little down about our lives and we make a snap decision.

You have a bad hair day and you cut your hair that you've been growing out for months.

You have a horrible day at work, so you eat an entire tub of ice cream, ruining your diet.

You blow your salary on clothes after a break up instead of putting it in your vacation savings account.

You send a nasty e-mail to a friend after a fight and end up not speaking to them for months.

Starting to see the picture?

Do you find yourself jumping from one fix to another, but never seem to be happy with your life? The problem with the gratification bounce is what goes up, must come down and often when we come down from a "happiness fix" our emotional state plummets to even new depths. This is when we have feelings of fear, doubt and become depressed and lethargic. Bouncing lowers our happiness curve and can even stagnate it. It is important to understand what your fixes are and learn how to avoid going down that path. Everybody has different ones, get to know yours and how to deal with them.

Happiness According To the Three Little Pigs

We all know the story about the three little pigs. With hair on their chins, they build their houses and a big bad wolf arrives. There's the entertainment value, but what is this story teaching children about happiness?

Three little pigs embark on a little DIY and build houses – two use inferior materials in order to get done faster and have fun. The third takes the time to plan out his house, select the right materials and carefully build his home because he knows it is an important part of his life. So the big bad wolf comes along and destroys the houses of the first two pigs while the third pig and his chinny-chin-chin sit safe and snug in his house.

Did you see the gratification bounce? The two pigs made a quick decision to build their houses in the fastest way possible, which leads to poor craftsmanship, so they can have fun sooner. Their world comes crashing down, quite literally, when the big bad wolf blows their houses down. Who knows what other carnage could have occurred due to this decision, most likely not fit for a children's tale.

Did you spot the proper HQC? The third little pig takes the time to plan out his house, using the correct materials and building practices, knowing it will take more time, but when the big bad wolf comes, he's safe and happy.

Enjoyment

Now that we understand how happiness works, let's get on to the real business of building your happiness. The first thing we are going to talk about is getting more enjoyment out of life. The connection between happiness and enjoyment is an important one. Isn't that the essence of a happy life, to enjoy every day?

The dictionary describes the word enjoy as: "to experience pleasure or happiness." So enjoyment is the active component of happiness. If you want to increase the pleasure and happiness you get out of each day you need to learn how to consistently enjoy life on a day to day basis.

Some people think that you can only enjoy life if you have money or a successful career or a loving partner, but that's not true. You can enjoy your life where you are and with what you already have. You can enjoy your life right now.

Do you see children waiting around for money or success to enjoy life? No, they embrace what they have today and enjoy it. Their day may be made by simply going to the park or building a fort. They take what they have now and use it to their advantage.

I'd like to share with you three tips that are essential to living a more enjoyable life today. Focus your efforts on these three simple tips and you will see an immediate impact in your life.

Tip 1: Break Routine

Enjoying life is about embracing change. However, humans are a contradiction of this because we are creatures of habit. Think about how you start your day. Do you not have the same routine? Do you drive the same roads to work? Do you go to the same restaurants, order the same foods off the menu? After awhile you feel like a hamster on a wheel. It is hard to find enjoyment in life when the routine is always the same. Life needs spice.

There's a phrase that says "if you continually do what you've always done, you'll continually get what you've always got." Why would you think your life is going to be any better, any more enjoyable if you do the same things you did yesterday, today? Boredom, routine and complacency are all enjoyment killers. They suck the life right out of you. When we get stuck in a rut by doing the same things over and over, enjoyment is out of reach.

We are always pushing children to try new things and thus have more enjoyable experiences. We buy them new toys, we take them to new places, and we encourage them to try new foods, play a new sport and so on. However, when was the last time that you tried something new?

How many times have you come home after a long day and just sat on the couch all night watching TV? At the end of the evening as you drag yourself off the couch to go to bed (if you haven't already fallen asleep on the couch!) you say something like: "What a waste of time. I had so many other things I could have done." We all do this from time to time, the frustrating part is when we come home the next day and the next and do it again. I can't even begin to tell you how many people have told me over the years that they just got stuck in this pattern and then didn't know how to break it and improve their lives.

14

In order to have more enjoyment in your life, you need to break the routines that have a negative pull on you and force yourself to make new decisions. It's like wiping the slate clean.

Let's use the TV zombie example. How do I break the routine of sitting on the couch and watching television so I can force a new decision? I shut off the television. It's that easy. Now I have a decision to make. Do I turn the one-eyed monster that's been sucking enjoyment out of my life back on or do I get off the couch and find something new I can do? In essence, by shutting the TV off, I force myself to make a new decision and now the ability to bring more enjoyment into my life rests with my next decision. Exciting, isn't it? It's not rocket science; people just get trapped in a routine and stop exercising their right to choose more enjoyment.

I bet at one time or another, a friend has called you up and asked you to go out, but you've been too tired to want to go. But that friend begged and cajoled until you finally said yes. At the end of the evening, did you end up saying something like, "We should do this more often."? You probably felt recharged and alive again. Why? Because you broke the routine that bound you. Imagine making choices like that every single day. You can. You just need to identify those routine traps that you fall into and make a conscious decision to avoid them.

I learned this skill early in my life from my parents. They taught me that the difference between a rut and a grave was merely the depth of the hole. If I was in a rut and wasn't enjoying life, they said I'd better do something about it because life is short and I can't get back the time I've lost.

Here are some easy ways to break routines that most people face every day and bring more enjoyment into your life.

Take the Road Not Travelled

Every day when you get up, you probably drive to work on the exact same road. Tomorrow, why not take a different route? In fact, take an extra fifteen minutes and see some new scenery on the way. Enjoy the new view.

Change It Up

Typically, we always go to the same restaurants all the time. In fact, many of us can probably quote what is on the menu and even tell you the prices because we order the same thing every time. Next time, try picking a number and then flip to the Yellow Pages and under Restaurants, count down the entries until you reach the number you picked. If you picked nine, you go to the ninth restaurant listed.

Take Action

If you are planning on going to a movie, instead of deciding based on your usual criteria (you like romantic comedies or drama films), go to the movie with the most amount of letters in the title. No matter what that movie is, go to it.

Why do you do this? Because it forces you to break routines and habits. You are able to experience new things. You may hit a dead end on your way home, the service at the restaurant may be horrible and the movie could be awful, but you did something completely different and therefore, you begin to see life just a little differently. You must learn to break your routines and force different choices if you truly want to experience the enjoyment life has to offer. If you don't do these things, you will never find the great park on the drive, the fantastic sushi restaurant or your new favorite movie.

What a Childhood Pet Can Teach Us about Happiness

As a child, chances are you had a goldfish that lived in a round goldfish bowl. The goldfish bowl had bright colored pebbles on the floor, a miniature castle and a little green plastic tree to one side. If you were really lucky, you had a tiny scuba man in there too. You fed your goldfish that flaky goldfish food and watched him swim around each day.

What you didn't realize is that every day your goldfish swam around his little bowl it was slowly making him blind. (It has been reported that round gold fish bowls cause fish to go blind over time. Some countries, including Rome, have banned them as cruelty to animals.)

Sometimes we are the goldfish. We are so used to swimming round and round that we become blind to the outside world and its possibilities. Our habits and routines stop us from seeing what is out there. We need to break free of the bowl.

Life teaches us lessons. It is up to us to learn them. Are you trapped in a goldfish bowl? What have you done lately to open your eyes to the opportunities that will allow you to break free? The biggest question of all is what are you willing to do today in order to have more enjoyment in your life? Make one decision today and another tomorrow and another the next day. What will you do differently?

Challenge yourself every morning to create one new action that you can implement to kick start your happiness. Share your idea with someone you trust if you need that extra incentive. But do it today. Don't wait. Every moment you don't consciously choose to break your routine and force those decisions to bring more enjoyment into your life is a moment lost that you can never, ever get back again. Don't do it for me. Do it because you want more happiness. As an extra bonus, if you choose to include the people most important to you, you can bring more enjoyment into their lives as well. Happiness and enjoyment tend to multiply with the more people you bring into the fold. They can also make sure that you don't fall back into your old ways and push you to continue to make positive changes in your life.

Tip 2: Appreciate What You Have

I can't emphasize enough how important this second tip is to life. No matter how many great things you do, if you don't learn to appreciate and be grateful for the smallest things in your life, you will always be open to seeing things negatively. If you learn to appreciate and be grateful for more of what you already have, you'll find yourself having more to enjoy.

The word "appreciate" has several different meanings. One is to be thankful or show gratitude. Another is to raise or increase in value, such as when you invest money in stocks or real estate. The value appreciates over time. I think that by being grateful for what we have in our lives, the things we have and want will also increase. In fact, they appreciate in value.

Many of us lead busy lives. We run from one event to another, trying to meet deadlines with customers, dropping off dry cleaning, cooking dinner and bathing kids. Sometimes just finding time to unload the dishwasher or take out the trash is difficult. Life these days can be hectic. It's easy to forget about the many things in life we have to be grateful for at the end of the day. They tend to be overshadowed by the stress of running. There's nothing wrong with being goal-driven, success-oriented people, but it is vitally important that we do not lose sight of the things that are most important to us, the things that are closest to our heart, the things we all too easily take for granted.

Let me ask you this: Did you know that your brain is hard-wired. It is conditioned to find whatever it looks for. Think about that for a moment. Whatever you look for, you find. Let me expand on this. Whenever I buy a new car, I always buy in the city I was born and raised. Although it is four hours away, I have dealt with the salesman for 20 years and completely trust him. When I buy a car, I always like to be unique. I want to be the guy that has that little something special that no one else in the area has yet. This makes my car easily identifiable when I need to find it in a packed Wal-Mart parking lot.

Years ago, when I was purchasing a new car, one of the deciding factors that influenced my decision was the color of the car. I had never seen it before and knew no one in the town I lived had a vehicle that color. I was so proud to drive it home. I took it out for a spin once I got there and much to my shock and displeasure, I saw a bunch of cars like mine in the exact same color. Why had I not seen these cars before? Because I wasn't looking for them. Once I knew what to look for, the cars magically appeared on the road.

The doctor comedy *Scrubs* takes this to a whole other level when Dr. Dorian fails to see women who are wearing wedding rings because he is not interested in speaking with women who aren't available. When they take off their wedding rings he is surprised to find Gift Shop Girl hasn't died at all, she just got engaged. When he bought flowers from her to send as a condolence to her family he didn't see her because he was no longer concerned with speaking to her due to her new status as "unavailable."

While it may not go as far as making people invisible, you and I, we're like that. If we wake up in the morning and expect to have a bad day, expect that someone will disappoint us, expect to not be happy, then that's exactly what we will get because our brains are hardwired to give it to us. We look for those situations that support what we are thinking. Conversely, if we expect to see great things, expect to have a great day, expect to find enjoyment then our brains will look for that as well.

What you choose to focus all your attention on tends to magnify it. If you focus on the problems in your life, they tend to increase. If you focus on the good things you already have, they too have a tendency to multiply. You must spend the time to appreciate those things in life that bring you enjoyment. Focusing on what you have and focusing on what you want, appreciates these things, and not only will they appear more abundantly, but they actually begin to grow. We will discuss in more depth how living a life of gratitude can bring you happiness further on.

Tip 3: Live in the Moment

Wayne Dyer, a terrific motivational speaker and author said, "When you dance, your purpose is not to get to a certain place on the floor, it's to enjoy each step along the way." If you don't live in the moment and are always rushing to the end, how can you get the most enjoyment out of what you're doing? By not living in the moment, you create the habit of jumping to the next "happiness fix" and creating a gratification bounce.

Sometimes it is our own impatience, our lack of taking the time to appreciate what we have and what we want that fuels a gratification bounce. We can become confused about what makes us happy by all this bouncing. By slowing down and living in the moment, it helps to eliminate the static noise that builds in our thoughts and creates more clarity around what really brings enjoyment to our lives.

Children are great at doing this. They never seem to be worrying about the future. For them, life is here and now. When children play, they are living in the moment. Play does not depend on the future; the past is merely used as fodder to make the play more interesting. This just comes naturally to children. As we become adults we lose this ability and end up spending too much of our time either living in the past or the future, rather than the present. Why do you think here and now is called the present? Because it is a gift. Be thankful for it.

Try this. Take a deep breath. Now take another one. Focus for a moment on just being in the moment. See, breathing is a great way to calm the mind and the body. Just simple deep breaths. As you take in another deep breath, think about today. Think about this instant. What are you truly grateful for? Don't think of the answers that society thinks is right, what others would want you to say. Think about you. What in your life right now brings you enjoyment? If you struggle to find answers to this question, you have some work to do. We have to ground ourselves in living in the moment, finding enjoyment with what we currently have in our lives so we can create the clarity and confidence to seek and do those things that truly make us happy versus reacting to the gratification bounce and putting our energy into the next "happiness fix." We must recondition our thoughts and our actions to create new habits to move us forward on our path to happiness.

I remember growing up and sitting around the dinner table and the inevitable question would pop up: "How was your day?" Despite the flak it has received over the years, this is a great question. It is meant to inform and to celebrate. However, in our busy lives, the answer to this question is often vague, if not outright negative. It can lead to minutes, sometimes hours of complaining about situations or people in our lives that brought misery to our day. Again, by focusing on what is wrong, we just invite more misery into our lives.

What if you put a condition on this question? What if you could only answer with what brought happiness and joy to your life that day? What if you could relive and appreciate what brought enjoyment to you that day, every day? What if your whole family had to answer that question every day around the dinner table? What if those closest to you got in the habit of answering this way? Would that one question alone bring more joy and happiness to your life? I can confidently tell you, yes, it would.

What a simple goal to work on this week. Can you commit to it? Can you commit to answering the question "How was your day?" and only include what you enjoyed that day? Whether you voice it around the dinner table, write it down in a journal or just spend a quiet moment and answer it for yourself, you will gain happiness and joy each day. This will help you appreciate life more and teach you how to live in the here and now.

Enjoyment is simply being in a state of joy. It is a decision that comes from within that affects our perceptions and our experiences of daily living. When you start out each day with the intention of enjoying life no matter what is going on around you, you become more in control. You become less reactive to things in your environment that may steal your happiness. Too often people let external circumstances dictate how they feel. If there's pressure and stress at work, they accept it and align with it. If someone close to them is negative and in a bad mood, they internalize it and take it personally. If their expectations aren't met, they blame someone else or get angry. Enjoyment of life is a choice. You just have to make it.

My father taught me that success is a split-second decision. He said it's all the agonizing that always takes so much time. We question whether we deserve to be happy. Don't agonize over the lack of enjoyment and happiness in your life. Don't waste any more time on the "what-ifs." Just make the decision to bring happiness and enjoyment into your life now.

These three tips are just the beginning of our journey to happiness. However, like all great journeys, they must begin with a single step. Bringing more enjoyment into your life is about changing the way you think and the habits you do every day. It doesn't take a lot of effort, but it does take commitment and a conscious effort to do things differently. You might find it easier to practice more enjoyment by focusing your time and attention on a couple of key areas.

Here are some ideas to start with:

Focus on the Positives

This sounds easy, but you have to really listen to the words you use and the situations that you find yourself in. Live in the moment and be fully aware of practicing positive behavior. Further on we will discuss how having a positive attitude will bring more happiness to your life.

Don't Judge

Don't be so judgmental of yourself or others. It is hard to focus on your own enjoyment when you are spending time and effort on being critical. Appreciating what you have and what others have to offer helps create a strong platform to build on. Your family and friends want more enjoyment in their lives as well; you need to help them find it.

Leave the Past in the Past

Release your resentments and practice forgiveness. Don't hold grudges. You can't build a life of enjoyment if there are negative feelings anchoring you to the past.

Enjoy the Simple Things

Taking the time to enjoy the little things life has to offer, like the warmth of the sun on your face, the birds singing while you're sitting on the deck, the comfort and love of holding someone's hand or the feeling of satisfaction when completing a task can bring much happiness to your life. By noticing and appreciating these things, you increase your capacity to look for and accept more enjoyment.

Look for Enjoyment

As simple as this sounds, ask yourself throughout the day, "What am I doing within this task right now that I enjoy?" Again, by looking for things and consciously asking yourself this question, you will find enjoyment in abundance.

Try Something New

Try something new that will bring you joy. It may be something you've always wanted to do, like play a round of golf or maybe something you used to do that brought joy to your life, such as a hobby, but that has been sacrificed because of other pressing needs.

My wife, Jane, and I took cooking classes together this year, not because we couldn't cook, but because we wanted to enjoy doing something together. By eliminating the noise of our day, it allowed us to spend quality time together while focusing our energy on learning something new about cooking. We made a decision to break our routine, to appreciate our relationship and to actually live in the moment which reinforced our enjoyment of each other.

You see, I know these principles of enjoyment work because I practice them as well. And if you practice them, over time joy will become a natural part of your everyday life. It's just a matter of choosing it, releasing any resistance and exploring ways to bring joy into every part of your life.

Before moving onto the next chapter, let's finish this off with words of advice from two famous people that sum up the topic discussed here.

Bruce Lee, the martial artist and actor, once stated that, "If you always put a limit on everything you do, physical or anything else, it will spread into your work and into your life. There are no limits. There are only plateaus and you must not stay there. You must go beyond them." Creating the right thoughts and habits are the first steps to going beyond your plateau.

And in the aspiration of being grateful for the simple things, an astute observation from a classic philosopher, who has taught generations of children how to enjoy life:

"Nobody can be un-cheered with a balloon."
-Winnie the Pooh

Happiness Obstacles

Action may not always bring happiness, but there is no happiness without action.

– Benjamin Disraeli

Chapter 2: Overcoming Your Fear

Our worst fear is not that we are inadequate. Our deepest fear is that we are powerful beyond measure. It is our light, not our darkness, that most frightens us. We ask ourselves, 'Who am I to be brilliant, gorgeous, talented, and fabulous?' Actually, who are you not to be? You are a gift of God, and you playing small doesn't serve the world. There's nothing enlightened about shrinking so that other people won't feel insecure around you. You were born to make manifest the glory of God within us. It's not just in some of us. It is in everyone. As we let our own light shine, we unconsciously give other people permission to do the same. As we are liberated from our own fear, our presence automatically liberates others.

- Marianne Williamson

When we look at what Williamson is saying, this is a powerful message. It implies that our fear can govern how great we become. Self-limiting thoughts stop us from achieving the more positive things in our life that we desire and hold us back from experiencing more happiness. But, by being the best we can be, we actually diminish our fear. We must break the barriers to let our light shine, not only for ourselves, but for others as well. By showing them how we

31

can embrace our full selves, we are giving them permission to do the same.

A Child's Perspective of Fear

Let's talk a little about fear itself. What is fear? To understand fear, I feel the need to tell you about the boy that lives next to me. This blond, mop-headed little guy is seven years old. He is just a ray of sunshine and he enjoys life. Through my open windows in the summer, I can hear him laughing as he races around on his little motorized jeep. He gets the most out of every moment whether it is digging holes in the background with his Tonka dump truck or "helping" his mother out in their garden. The big reason I want to introduce you to him is because of his approach to life – he has no fear. Remember how we said that children find more happiness in life because they haven't discovered fear yet? This boy exemplifies that. He loves to catch anything, be that scaly fish from the river, spotted frogs, withering snakes, hairy spiders, slimy salamanders or squishy bugs.

The other day while I was standing on the deck having an ice tea, I saw him catching bees in his butterfly net. Can you imagine? *Bees!* If he sees a garter snake crawl under a rock, he will stick his tiny hand in there and pull it out. He'll catch three or four of them at a time and then, get this; he will put them into his kiddie pool and swim with them! He literally swims with these snakes. When was the last time you did something so fearless as to swim with snakes? Just touching a snake would put many people in a panic, let alone swimming with them in a little pool.

This summer, he decided it was time to jump off the high tower of our dock into the river. Just so you understand, the high tower is a twenty foot drop into the water and this little boy is only four feet high and about 50 lbs. But he was determined, so I told him "Keep your legs together, point your toes and enjoy the jump." Did he hesitate? Did he quiver at the sight of that plummet? No, with a big smile on his face he just did it. This scrawny kid jumped off that tower with such incredible excitement. And he wasn't satisfied with doing it only once, he did it again and again and again.

Fear is a learned behavior. Children are not daunted by things that would stop many adults short because they haven't learned to fear the world around them. A child wants to touch the flame of a candle because they have yet to learn it will harm them. They see only its beauty and want to hold it themselves. Once fear has developed it can and will rob you of your enjoyment of life. If we give into our fears and start paying attention to them, they become self-fulfilling prophecies. Your fear prevails. The good news is, if fear is a learned behavior, then it can be unlearned and we can retrain ourselves so our fears no longer own us.

Just imagine going through life like my seven year old neighbor where he looks at everything as an opportunity for joy and wonderment instead of letting fear hold him back. We were all like that at one time in our lives. Your goal now is to figure out what that felt like and go back to those kinds of thoughts and actions.

A few years back, my wife and I were shopping in a mall when from behind a rack of clothes a woman stepped out and said, "Hey! Remember me? You taught me how to golf." Now, I've worked with a lot of people over the years and taught them how to do many different things, but I've never taught someone how to golf! But I did remember her. She was in a class I taught on presentation skills.

"Of course I remember you, Cathy. I taught you how to give presentations, not how to golf," I laughed.

She smiled and said something remarkable. "Because I was able to get over my fear of public speaking, which is supposed to be one of the biggest fears adults have, I had the courage to try golfing." You see, Cathy had always wanted to golf, but was afraid of making a fool of herself. Once she saw that she could overcome one of her largest fears, she decided that she could overcome any of them. She changed the way she looked at fear. Now she's joined a women's league and has increased her enjoyment. By facing one of our fears, we can gain happiness in other areas of our lives.

What are you missing out on in your life because of a fear? Let's rephrase that, what would you be doing if you had no fear? Remember, fear is a learned behavior. We are not born into this world with fear. We were born with hope, love and joy. Fear is what we learned over time. It is social conditioning. As children we were wide-eyed, adventurous and open to new ideas. Over time, as we watched those around us responding to different situations with fear and anxiety, we assumed we were supposed to react this way as well. In essence, we began to mimic them.

My wife does not like thunderstorms. The closer the storm; the louder the cracks of thunder; the more blinding the lightning; the more anxiety she feels. When our children were younger, I began to notice that they too quickly became afraid of thunderstorms by watching their mother's reaction. To combat this, when a thunderstorm would come rolling across the river, I would take them out onto the screened porch. Kneeling down beside them, whenever thunder boomed or lightning streaked across the sky, I would say "Wow! Isn't that a great noise?" or "That's amazing, look at the light show!" Eventually, they conquered their fear and now enjoy a good thunderstorm. The outcome? A learned behavior of fear was unlearned. They were retrained so that now a thunderstorm is something to marvel.

Fears Defined

So what are we afraid of? What motivates fear? If you look in any psychology text book you will find page upon page of things people fear: achluophobia (fear of darkness), catoptrophobia (fear of mirrors), koniophobia (fear of dust), omphalophobia (fear of bellybuttons).

However, in my experience with people and how much enjoyment they get from their lives, it usually narrows down to four areas: failure, rejection, the unknown and success.

Fear of Failure

Fear of failure is ingrained in all of us from the time we hit school. We are given tests and grades, we pass or fail, we win or lose. Life should not be viewed the same way, but many of us do see it this way. Where would we be if people stopped trying because of a fear of failure? Think of all the great breakthroughs in life that came after someone pushed past failure.

You need to have an attitude of failing forward. There's nothing wrong with failing. It's called a life lesson. You have to learn from this lesson so you don't make the same mistakes. In essence, you need the failure to take you forward in your development. The early 20th century actor, Ilka Chase said "The only people who never fail are those who never try." Failure shouldn't be feared; it should be embraced when it happens and used to push you forward. You should view it as a tool, not a hindrance. When you begin to see failure in this manner, you will be far more willing to try new activities that may bring new happiness into your life. Happiness you would not have discovered had you let your fear of failure stop you.

Fear of Rejection

Often when I coach people facing the fear of rejection, I remind them of the wise words of Eleanor Roosevelt. She said, "No one can make you feel inferior without first getting your consent." Do not go out in the world and let other people dictate what you do. By doing this, you are handing over control of your happiness. Why should someone else be in control of your happiness? Not everyone is going to like you or what you do. That is just a fact of life. The true tragedy is when you let this hinder your growth.

Fear of the Unknown

There are many things in the world that are unknown, but just because they are unknown doesn't mean you should fear them. Remember, before your best friend was your friend, they were a stranger. An unknown author described fear as false evidence appearing real. Often we attach situations with negative subtexts they do not deserve. Look beyond the fear and you will begin to see that the unknown is just something waiting to be known. Nothing more, nothing less.

Fear of Success

The last fear, the fear of success, is the one that always surprises me. People are afraid to try new things, to break those self-limiting behaviors because, if they succeed, people will always expect them to perform at this new level and they fear they will let people down by not being able to do so. Like Williamson said at the beginning of this chapter, people are afraid of their light, of how great they can be.

People all over the world are leading dull, boring lives because they are held captive by their own self-imposed limitations. They have built the walls of their own prisons and are now forced to stay there. They are both the inmate and the warden. Do people want to live like this? Do you want to live this way? My experience tells me no. People just struggle with breaking the habits that jail them. Life conditioning has defined in their minds what they can do and what they deserve from life.

What limiting beliefs do you struggle with? Do you have excuses as to why you're not enjoying life? Listen to your words. Do you say any of the following?

"I'm too old or too young."
"I'm not good enough."
"I lack the knowledge."
"I don't have the time."
"I don't have the money."
"I'll never be able to do that."

While there may be a hint of truth in some of these statements, these are still limiting beliefs that control your thoughts, emotions and actions, thus impacting your ability to enjoy new experiences. You must reshape the way you view your fears through your thoughts, emotions and actions in order to gain more control and happiness in life. All of these areas are connected. Think of something you've always wanted to do, but due to your self-limiting beliefs or fears, you chose not to do it. Why did you choose not to do this? Because your belief governed your thoughts which fed your emotions which limited or controlled your actions (or lack of actions), which impacted any experience you might have had.

If I want to learn how to ride a horse because my family is going on a vacation where there is horseback riding excursions on the beach, but I already don't think I can do it before I get there, what do you think is going to happen? If I go to a riding lesson and I'm already thinking I can't do it, when I get on my horse, my doubt in my own ability will feed into my fear of the horse. I'm going to panic. My heart will race. I'll tense up. I'm not going to enjoy myself and thus I'm going to have a hard time learning how to ride the horse. I have confirmed my own self-limiting beliefs. I am my own self-fulfilling prophecy.

You need to consciously make decisions rather than the usual unconscious reactive ones. If you change your thoughts about your abilities, you impact your emotions. If your emotions are more positive, then your actions will be more confident. This will increase your overall enjoyment and the happiness you will derive out of situations.

"Fraidy Shark, Fraidy Shark"

One of my colleagues, Renée, recently had a baby. When my wife and I were picking out a gift to send to them we decided to add a couple children's books. One of them, by Brian James, was called *The Shark Who Was Afraid of Everything!*

One day the book caught my eye where it was sitting on the dining room table waiting to be dropped off. I decided to flip through it because it reminded me of the stories I used to read my kids. As I looked at the colorful drawings and the catchy rhymes, the story made me pause. In this simple child's book was a lesson on overcoming our fears.

The story goes that there was once a shark named Sharky who lived under the sea with all the other sharks. However, Sharky was different from all the others because he was afraid of everything: the whales with great big tales, the ships with little sails. You get the point. And all the other sharks would chant "'fraidy shark, 'fraidy shark." Despite being afraid of so many things, Sharky most feared that all the other sharks might be right. Do you see where I'm going here? Sharky let his fears dictate his life. He let what the other sharks thought of him control what he did. Sharky was so unhappy that he ran away. When he did so, Lily the little fish went with him. Distracted from his own self-limited thoughts and those of others, Sharky began to enjoy himself.

Sharky and Lily end up getting lost and Lily becomes scared. Knowing he must do something to help his friend, Sharky tells her not to be scared, that he will find their way back. When put into a situation that forces Sharky to change his way of thinking and acting, Sharky forgets he is afraid of everything and ends up being the bravest of them all.

This story teaches children that they need not let fear of what others say limit what they do. They need to change their thoughts and actions in order to overcome their fears and find happiness.

Changing Your View of Fear

So how *do* you change these thoughts? First, you have to acknowledge your fear. Acknowledge it for what it is and that it actually exists. Second, you need to understand the message that you're telling yourself. Be open to the possibility that it is limiting you. Look at it honestly and critically to see what impact it is having on your life. Find out what thoughts are behind this fear. Often, the root of most performance fears is "I'll fail" or "They won't like me." Third, control your thoughts and emotions around the fear. Don't let it control your anxiety by focusing on the worst case scenario or the "what-if-this-happens" fear mongering mentality. Fourth and most importantly, intentionally change the thoughts you have about the situation. Use words and mental pictures that have positive outcomes. What's the ideal outcome of this event? What would you like to happen? What would make you happy? Mark Twain said, "Courage is resistance to fear, mastery of

41

fear, not absence of fear. Do the thing you fear most and the death of fear is certain."

I'm a firm believer that life presents us with many lessons and it's up to us to learn them. In Africa, lions feed on gazelles. They love gazelle meat. The problem arises from the fact that gazelles are very fast and difficult to catch. To compensate for this, a group of young lions act as sheepdogs and herd the gazelles towards a pre-determined location. The gazelles easily outrun the young lions, but what they don't realize is that in the deep, grassy area they are running into, a group of older lions is hiding. These lions are too old to be part of the chase and don't stand a chance of catching their own meat. However, they are particularly good at roaring. When the gazelles come close enough to the older lions, they leap out of the grass and roar loudly. The gazelles immediately panic, responding to the perceived fear of imminent death, and run away from the older lions that could never catch them, right into the waiting jaws of the young lions.

There are many roaring situations in life. Are they real or are they perceived? Obviously, the real roaring fear you must be careful of. The roaring fears of self-limitations are the ones you must respond to, understand, grapple with and then throw down. You must acknowledge that they exist, understand them and then consciously change your thinking around each and every one. A simple way to do this is to write them down. Think of something that you avoid doing because of fear; it could be giving presentations, learning to

42

ski or getting on a plane. Once you have it, make two lists. On the first one, list all the negative limiting thoughts you have and the fears and worries you've associated with this activity. On the second list, write out the positive outcomes possible by partaking in this activity. List the things you would like to see happen. Create a mental picture of what would make you happy.

Now, look at the first list. Ask yourself if these things are even possible? Often when we see our fears written on paper we start to see how unreasonable they are. However, sometimes are fears are grounded in truth. If this is the case, take a look at your second list. Circle the most positive outcomes for you, the ones that would make you most happy. Is it really worth letting the fears on your first list stop you from achieving the happiness on your second list? No, so to get yourself moving, write down three actions to move you towards achieving these positive outcomes. See the fear of flying example on the next page for help getting started.

After writing out your actions, post them up so they are visible to you every day. You conquer your fears by facing your fears. By constantly looking beyond your self-limiting thoughts, it gives you clarity, direction and confidence to face them each day. You see what is draining you of happiness and what can give you joy.

As a child, do you remember lying in bed worried about monsters? You were afraid of a boogeyman coming out of the closet or that maybe something was hiding under your

Fear of Flying Example

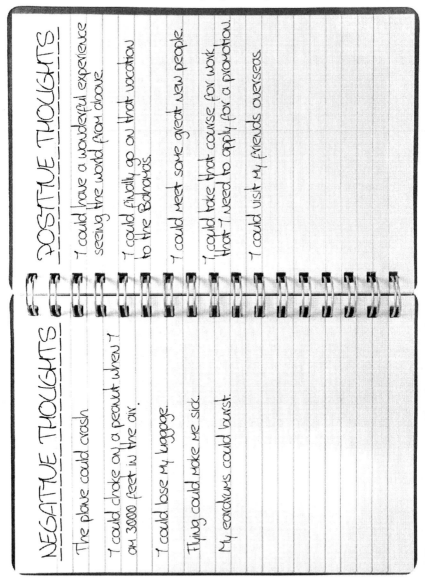

NEGATIVE THOUGHTS

The plane could crash.

I could choke on a peanut when I am 30000 feet in the air.

I could lose my luggage.

Flying could make me sick.

My eardrums could burst.

POSITIVE THOUGHTS

I could have a wonderful experience seeing the world from above.

I could finally go on that vacation to the Bahamas.

I could meet some great new people.

I could take that course for work that I need to apply for a promotion.

I could visit my friends overseas.

bed? Your nightlight cast strange shadows and you were sure night noises were coming from monsters outside your window. Even though there was nothing there, the fear was real for you. You hid under the covers while your heart pounded. Usually at some point, a parent came into your room, turned on the light and opened the closet door and checked under the bed just to show you there was nothing there. Maybe, if you were an especially courageous little kid, you slipped out of bed yourself and checked under it or in the closet. Either way, you found out there was nothing there but a few dust bunnies or your clothes. The fear was just a perceived one. It was all in your mind. Many times, fear and self-limiting beliefs are all creations of our imaginations. And when we start shining the light of reason under the beds and into the closets where these fears live, we discover there is nothing there at all.

Fear is overrated. Fear has no reality other than the one you choose to give it. By acknowledging your fears and planning for them, you will be liberated from them. Start redirecting the attention and time you give to creating fear towards more positive thoughts and the fear will diminish and your enjoyment and happiness will increase. The bars of your prison will disappear and you will gain control over your life again.

Chapter 3: Finding Your Motivation

The largest waterfall begins with a single drop of water and great results in your life come from taking that first step. But what if you don't know where to start or even what to get started on? Motivation is defined as "to give reason, incentive, enthusiasm or interest that causes specific action or certain behavior." All motivation is self-motivation. No one can force motivation on you. You must decide what you want and decide that you will take action to get it or nothing will happen. This applies to happiness in your life as well. If you aren't motivated to make the changes to bring more happiness and enjoyment into your life, then you won't get it.

People ask me all the time about motivation. They say they struggle with it, both finding it and keeping it. They have no energy at the end of the day to exercise. They tell me about their team at work that's not productive. They say that their son or daughter lies around the house all day and does absolutely nothing. First of all, let me make a bold statement. There is no such thing as a motivation problem. That's right. Anyone can get motivated whenever they choose to be motivated. You just need desire, a burning "why." The focus is on the reasons why not to change versus why you should.

Routine, boredom and doubt are all killers to the motivation you need to be happy. We are creatures of habit and, thus, form tired, safe routines as we discussed in the first chapter. We lull ourselves into complacency. Think about how routine chips away at your awareness, the enjoyment you get out of life.

Have you ever had to drive long distances, maybe 45 or 60 minutes one way, for a period of time? I had a client where I had to drive over an hour one way to every day for a couple of months. There was only one road to take and I quickly dreaded the drive. I remember how my wife used to call me on my cell phone and ask where I was; what time should she expect me home. And I would say, "Jane, you know what? I don't know." She wondered how I could not know where I was, but because of the monotony of the drive I would forget whole periods of time, whether I went through a certain town or passed a crossroad. The drive left me feeling drained and frustrated. You need change in your life. You need to break routine if you want to feel joy and to do this you must find motivation.

Action Reaction

Let me ask you a question: What do you feel comes first, action or motivation? Most people tell me motivation. They feel you have to be motivated before you can take action. This isn't always the truth. Sometimes it is action that drives our motivation.

Have you ever awoken on a Saturday and known you had to get the house clean, but just didn't feel like doing it? You decided that you would do a little vacuuming instead of the full cleaning you planned. But before you knew it you'd moved from the vacuuming to the dusting to cleaning the bathroom and washing the floors. By starting with a little action, you became motivated to get the job done.

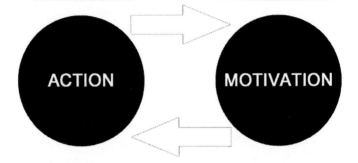

While most people don't enjoy cleaning their house and need help getting motivated to do it, this goes for things that you'd like to do as well, but just can't seem to get motivated to do. Maybe you'd like to learn a new sport like tennis, but haven't been able to find the drive. You keep giving yourself excuses: I don't have the time; I'm not in good enough shape; I don't have a racquet. What if you just put all that aside, and chose to pick up the phone and call to inquire about lessons? That's it. Just one call. What do you think would happen? You might find out that they have a day of the week that works perfectly for you. You might get excited and buy a racquet. You might go to the first lesson and find out you are in good enough shape. And you might just love it and keep going. Do you see how one action can give you the motivation to go out and do so much more? Action leads to motivation which leads to more action.

George Washington Carver once said, "Ninety-nine percent of failures come from people who have the habit of making excuses." You can make the choice to have more motivation in your life by simply choosing to act. One act can start the ball rolling towards an avalanche of motivation.

You have choices like this every single day. You have them in the morning and the evening; you have them at work and at home on the weekend. You need to look at the routine you're in and ask yourself what action you need to take to increase your motivation. The power you get from taking action is eye-opening and rewarding. It raises your confidence and self-esteem. It stimulates energy and knocks down the walls of doubt and fear. Action puts control and momentum into your hands. Bear in mind the phrase "idle hands are the work of the devil." If you have too much time on your hands, it's easier to stew over why you aren't succeeding or why you're not happy.

Five Steps to Generating Motivation

There are five steps that can take you from stalled on your journey to "someday" by routine to having the motivation necessary to propel you towards more happiness in your life. They are simple to implement and will have a huge impact on your life.

Step One

Remember I said there is no such thing as a motivation problem; that anyone can get motivated. You just need a reason. To create a reason, you first need to become aware of the routine in your life. You need to acknowledge the boredom and the mundane present in your life and find a reason to change it. This can be done by an internal decision to succeed or an external factor that influences change. We produce an internal decision to change simply because we want to. You look at your situation and say you're tired of it and you want more. You want more excitement. You want to feel alive. This is about making a decision from the inside out.

External factors can also generate awareness, but you have to put yourself in a situation where you can be exposed to them. This means, that while you might not feel motivated, you have to take the action of dragging yourself out of the house and experiencing something different. Go to a movie, take a hike in the woods, or go to a community event. If you're feeling less motivated at work then take a seminar, join a service club, or form a walking club where you can discuss things with other people. These will expose you to external factors where new ideas and experiences are fully enjoyed. Take in everything from these and then ask yourself: What can I do with this? If you take the time to think it through, trust me when I tell you, motivation will strike.

Step Two

Have you ever had an AH HA experience? One where you thought, "I can do this." Often you'll get them after being stuck in a rut for a while. You get that feeling deep down that says, "I'm ready for change." When this happens, you need to start opening yourself up to ideas around you and one day you will get an idea and you will want to do it. You will know it is the one thing that will help you climb out of your rut. The key is being able to recognize and embrace it.

Step Three

This step is all about action. Being excited doesn't create results. Only action produces results. Merely thinking about your "someday" and what would bring you happiness doesn't make it happen. Walt Disney built the place near and dear to every child's heart (young and old) and the number one travel destination in the world and it was all based on four words: dream, believe, dare and do. As you gain belief in your dreams, you must dare yourself to do different things every day to make them a reality. You must commit yourselves to doing. You can't back down just because it scares you. Remember, if you continually do what you've always done, you'll continually get what you've always got. When you've identified what brings you motivation and know where you want to go, you need to put in sufficient time and energy to bring it to fruition. Disney understood that true greatness came from doing this every day, ingraining it in your thoughts and actions.

Step Four

Now that you're acting, you need to start keeping track of the results. This stage is about making sure you get things done. You need to check things off your list. We thrive on accomplishments and thus your confidence is directly tied to the success that you have in your tasks. If you get in the habit of finishing tasks then this will bring more satisfaction and happiness to your life.

Think about it. Do you ever write To Do lists? Do you find that your satisfaction in a day is tied to your ability to fulfill the tasks on the list? If you had ten things on your list and by two in the afternoon you had nine finished, you'd probably feel good about that day. However, if at the same time you had only one or two tasks finished, wouldn't you be disappointed and frustrated, not only about that day, but about the next one that is already filling up with today's work?

You need to make a conscious effort to continually remind yourself that you are succeeding. If you do not check off your accomplishments; if you do not complete things on a daily basis, then you accept frustration into your life. Celebrate the little victories as they come along and your journey will be more enjoyable.

Step Five

Now that you are creating excitement through your successes, you need to reward yourself. You need to pat yourself on the back. Treat yourself. Make yourself a deal at the first step that if you complete a task or reach your goal, you are going to buy a new sweater or take yourself out for a great dinner. It is important that you reward your efforts and achievements because this is what motivation flourishes on. This is what happiness grows from.

The Little Train That Could

We all know that classic children's story about the little train that could. It was told to us many times by many different people. When we didn't think we could ride our bike without training wheels, our parents reminded us of the engine. When we didn't believe we could master long division in school, our teacher brought him up. When we just didn't imagine we could ever hit the ball in little league, our coach told us to say "I think I can, I think I can" while we stood at the base waiting for the ball. And you know what? We learned how to ride a two wheeler, we figured out how to do long division (even if we don't remember now), and we ran excitedly to first base after hitting a grounder.

The magic of the *Little Train That Could* is that it covers all five steps to gaining motivation. It's true. In case you've forgotten the story, an early version goes as follows:

A little railroad engine worked at a station yard pulling cars on and off the switches. It wasn't a big, important job, but he did it well. One morning, as he was waiting for the next call, a long train of freight cars asked a large engine to take it over the big hill by the yard. While this was what the large engine was made for, he still replied, "I can't. You have too much for me to pull." The train then asked another engine who also said no. He asked every capable engine in the yard only to be refused by them all with varying excuses. Finally, with no one else to turn to, the train asked the little engine if he could pull him up over the hill. "I think I can," declared the little train and without hesitation he moved to the front of the large train and started up the hill. As he climbed, he kept bravely puffing, "I think I can, I think I can, I think I can."

As he neared the top of the hill, which had discouraged so many of the bigger engines, he began to slow down. Undeterred, he kept saying, "I—think—I can, I—think—I—can." Using his strong sense of conviction, he made it to the top. As he went down the other side, he congratulated himself by saying, "I thought I could, I thought I could!"

In the first step the little engine was in a situation that presented an external factor to motivate it to look beyond its regular routine of pulling cars on and off switches to a much bigger goal of pulling the large train of freight cars.

Next, despite all the other trains saying they can't do it, the little locomotive says he thinks he can, achieving Step Two.

54

He moves into Step Three by taking the action of putting himself in front of the train and pulling him up the hill.

He keeps track of his accomplishments as he reaches the top of the grade and takes it more slowly. And at the end he congratulates himself.

There is a commonality that each one of these steps shares that you can see in the little train story as well. It is choice. Each of these steps is about choosing to take control and move to the next one. At any point, if you do not take control of the step, you will fall back and instead of riding the wave of motivation, you will be left behind to drown in a life of monotony.

Choose to believe in yourself. Choose to find more happiness in your life. Choose to "think you can."

Finding What Makes You Happy

The world stands aside to let anyone pass
who knows where he is going.
– David Starr Jordan

Chapter 4: Discovering Your Life Purpose

Do you believe you have a purpose? Many people play around with the idea of what their life purpose is, but they fail to ask themselves if they actually believe they have one. Most don't even give this much thought. But what would it mean to you to have a clear purpose in life? Wouldn't you be happier knowing you were working towards something you believed in?

Most of us are busy doing what we think we have to do. Our days are packed with expectations from work, family and the pressures of society and we don't even think about what *we* want to do. As creatures of habit we go about our days not questioning why we do the things we do. We create routines and fall into the trap of doing the same things, the same way, at the same time, each and every day.

Many unhappy or bored people describe their lives to me as robotic. Other than a few deliberate changes to the mix, such as a vacation or a buying a new toy, life is predictable. This often causes people to wonder if this is all there is to life. There are even people out there that have great lives, but tell me they have a nagging feeling of not being happy and fulfilled. These are people who are doing things they enjoy, but they are seeking more from life. "More" isn't monetary, it's a deep-down-in-the-gut feeling that lets you know something is lacking in your life. That "something" is a clearly defined purpose.

I have a friend who once said that many people talk about finding themselves, but in reality, your life is not something you go out and find. It's something you create. These words have stuck with me over the years. You *create* your life. No excuses. No blame. I am responsible for creating my own life. My choices. My decisions. My actions. My way.

You're wondering if it can be that simple. It is, but you need to slow down and take stock of your life first. One day a very keen and eager master martial artist approached Bruce Lee and asked him to share his knowledge and wisdom and teach him everything he knew about martial arts. Lee's response was to hold up two cups, filled to the top with water. He said the first cup represented all the knowledge his eager companion knew about martial arts. The second cup was filled with all of Lee's knowledge. Lee said, "If you want to fill your cup with my knowledge, you must empty your cup of your knowledge."

My dream in life was to become an entrepreneur and I am one. My goal was to define success on my own terms and I do. However, for many years I was running full out, jumping from one project to the next, flying from one client to another, constantly creating new opportunities to be at the top of my game. I was bolting after my dream of success and money. The problem was I was so caught up in running that I had forgotten why I was running. Do you find yourself doing this? If you're not careful, you can get consumed with all this running.

To truly uncover your purpose in life you need to slow down and be willing to empty your mind, or your cup, of all the negative messages and distractions you've adopted over the years. You need to stop running and take a breather.

The Personal Mission Statement

Remember the movie *Jerry Maguire*? Tom Cruise played the lead role of an agent that was overwhelmed by his life and came to the realization that he had lost sight of what was important to him. Do you remember the turning point in the movie? He actually sat down and wrote out a personal mission statement. He identified what his purpose was and he used it to start his own business and redirect where his life was taking him.

You may think real people don't do things like this, it just looks good in movies, but I saw the results of this approach in action this year. My wife and I attended the retirement party of a principal she used to work with. Brian was an incredible principal, every day he used to go down and read to the kindergarten students. He truly cared about what he did. During his farewell speech, he talked about how rewarding his career had been, some of the highlights and the lessons he'd learned over the years. Then he went on to talk about a lesson he'd learned at the beginning of his career that was now being culminated at this party. He said that

61

when he first became a principal, a friend and fellow principal said that he should imagine himself at his retirement party. What would he want his family, friends and peers to say about him that day? Brian took this to heart and wrote down what he wanted and read it every day. He let these words drive his thoughts and his actions. This became his purpose in life. And sitting there at his retirement party, listening to the praise, admiration and acclaim lavished upon this man, there was no question in my mind that he created his life.

What about your life? Have you given it much thought lately? Imagine being at your own retirement party surrounded by family, friends and co-workers. There's excitement in the air as people prepare themselves to stand at the podium and speak in your honor. The moment of truth arrives. Imagine the words you would hear. What are the most important things you would want them to say? What would your lifetime achievements be? What would matter most to you? Now ask yourself if you are doing these things right now. Are your actions today leading to what you want to hear at your retirement? You may not think that what you do today matters, but purpose is about choosing to make a difference on your terms each and every day.

Many years ago I heard this story and I've shared it with people ever since. It's a story about starfish. A writer had rented a cottage at the seashore one summer. Early one morning he decided to walk on the beach for inspiration. As he walked, he saw a figure in the distance that appeared to be dancing in the waves. As he approached, he realized the figure was a little girl. And as he got even closer, he found that the girl wasn't dancing, but retrieving something off the beach. As he got close enough to see clearly, he realized the young girl was picking up starfish, running lightly through the waves, and tossing them gently over the breakers into the sea. When he was in speaking distance, he asked the girl what she was doing. The girl paused in her actions and said that the starfish had washed ashore during the night and if left on the sand, they would die.

"I'm returning the starfish to the sea," she said and then, yet again, reached down, picked up another starfish and ran through the waves, gently returning it to the sea.

The writer looked around at the beach dotted with starfish and was perplexed.

"There are miles and miles of beach and thousands upon thousands of starfish stranded on the sand. How can you possibly think that you can make a difference?"

The young girl proceeded to the next starfish. She reached down and picked it up, ran lightly through the waves and gently tossed the starfish into the sea. When she returned to the beach, she looked into the writer's eyes and responded quietly, "I made a difference to that one."

Defining a purpose is about making a difference on your own terms.

When you first think about mission statements, you initially may not connect them with your personal life. You most likely think about them as belonging in the work world.

Chances are, at some point in time, you've been involved in an organizational meeting to define a mission statement for your company or department. Mission statements provide direction and purpose for companies and guide the actions and decisions of people within that company. They answer the question, "What business are we in?" Are these not the same things you need in your life? Does it not make sense that there is value in spending time creating a personal mission statement? While they will obviously serve different purposes, the fundamental principles are the same. A personal mission statement describes what you want to focus on, what you want to accomplish and who you want to become in a specific area of your life. This helps you focus your thoughts, energy, behaviors, and actions towards the things that are most important to you.

There are many different approaches to creating a personal mission statement. Before I share these with you, let's look at guidelines you should consider while designing your statement. Reflect on these five guideposts:

First and foremost, it must be motivational and it must be yours. Your words should reflect what you want to focus on and your passion for the person you want to become.

Second, a personal mission statement must grow with you over time. It represents where you are now and who you will be over the next one to three years. As your situation changes, a new personal mission statement must emerge as well.

Third, don't worry about length. Your statement can be short or long, whatever makes sense to you and motivates you. The best mission statements are the ones that you can state without having to look them up again.

Fourth, to be truly effective, you should make it part of your daily life. Mine, which I'll share with you shortly, is on my wall above my desk at work. I also have it written in my journal where I reflect on it during downtimes.

Finally, because your purpose in life impacts those around you, your personal mission statement should take into consideration how your actions, thoughts and behaviors affect the important relationships in your life.

Everyone has a different preference when it comes to creating a personal mission statement. You must choose the one the best suits your personality.

The Easy Way

The simplest approach is more informal and less structured. It requires you to do the following: find a quiet place to think with a piece of paper and a pen (or in front of your computer). At the top of your paper write these questions:

Why do I exist?
What is my purpose in life?

Write all the answers that come into your head. Don't worry about making it perfect or pretty. Just write it all down as it comes to you. Now, review your answers and write out clearer ones based on them. For everything you've written down, ask yourself, "Is this my true purpose?" Keep repeating this until you get that tug on your heart, the one thing that makes you say, "I've got it." Don't expect it to jump off the page at you right away. Sometimes you need to be patient and keep reworking it. See the next page for an example of what this might look like when completed. You can choose to follow this format or use a different way that suits you better.

If you've been developing a personal mission statement for a while, then this activity may only take you 15 to 20 minutes. However, if you struggle with purpose in your life, it could take you longer. You will know when you've found it because you will feel an emotional connection to the words that you've written down.

The Building Blocks of Personal Mission Statements

You may need a more structured approach to developing your statement. This method begins the same as the last with finding a quite place away from interruptions with your writing implements. However, instead of writing whatever comes into your head, I want you to answer the nine questions below. I want you to put down the first thing that

Example of a Personal Mission Statement Activity

<u>Why do I exist?</u>
<u>What is my purpose in life?</u>

Wife   Mother   Daughter   Sister
        Employee   Colleague   Friend

love   support   teach   raise   remember   help
        make a difference   have fun

To be a good, loving wife.

To support my family and always be there for them.

To raise my daughter to the best of my ability, teaching her how to be a good person and showing her the world.

To use my creativity and intelligence at work.

To have fun and enjoy myself!

comes into your head. Don't over think your answers. Be completely honest.

Question 1: What makes you happy?

Question 2: What have you really enjoyed doing in the past and what do you really enjoy doing now?

Question 3: What makes you feel absolutely great about yourself?

Question 4: Whom do you admire? What qualities do you most admire in this person?

Question 5: What is missing from your life that you've always wanted to do?

Question 6: What is most important to you in your life right now?

Question 7: What values do you hold dear? Which ones are the most important to you?

Question 8: If you had a message to leave for this world, what would it be?

Question 9: If you could apply your knowledge and talents anywhere, what would you do?

Once you've written the answers down on paper, you've now created the foundation of your personal mission statement. All you need to do is complete the following four steps.

Step One: With the answers from the questions in front of you, circle all the action words that you connect with on a higher level, words like empower, inspire, motivate, improve, teach or guide.

Step Two: Write down everyone and everything that you believe you can impact because of these actions, whether it is people, nature, organizations, special interest groups or others.

Step Three: Identify your desired outcome. How will your actions benefit these groups? What is your end goal?

Step Four: Combine the various answers from Steps One to Three together into one sentence or a couple sentences. Remember, this might take some time, so don't get frustrated if it doesn't happen in the first ten minutes. Just keep playing with your words and set up until they jump off the page and grab you by the shirt collar. Don't rush it. This is an important step to developing your statement. You may need to walk away for a while and revisit it later to get a better perspective.

Once you have your one or two sentences, make sure you can see yourself getting up every day and fulfilling those words. They need to drive your life with purpose. It may take time to create it, but it will be some of the best time that you could ever invest in yourself.

Now that you have your mission statement, don't just put it in a drawer. Display it where you can see it every day and make sure to read it often. Since your statement describes your unique purpose in life, by reviewing it daily, it becomes a benchmark by which you live. It grounds you in times of turmoil. It anchors you in times of insecurity. It also becomes the bounce in your step every morning and the confidence and clarity in your actions throughout the day. Each night you can go to sleep knowing that you are doing what you mean to do with your life. If you want more security, inspiration, success and happiness in your life, defining your purpose is the best way to start.

The Personal Mission Statement of
the Velveteen Rabbit

Don't laugh, it's true! The Velveteen Rabbit had a personal mission statement. Not only did he have a mission statement, despite all odds, he fulfilled it.

You all remember the story *The Velveteen Rabbit*, by Margery Williams. The Boy is given the Velveteen Rabbit as a Christmas gift and he lives in the Boy's nursery. The Velveteen Rabbit wishes to be Real and the Skin Horse tells him that to be Real, a child must really and truly love him.

The little Velveteen Rabbit becomes the Boy's constant companion and eventually becomes old and tattered. One day the Boy becomes ill with scarlet fever and when he gets better the Velveteen Rabbit is replaced. The happy ending is that the Nursery Fairy comes along and makes him into a real live rabbit.

So, what was the Velveteen Rabbit's personal mission statement? He wanted to become Real by being loved by a child. His entire life was devoted to making the Boy love him. Despite the fact that his coat became shabby, his nose rubbed off and he lost his stuffing, he kept with it.

Sure, he doubted himself at times, especially when he met live rabbits and they told him he couldn't be Real because he couldn't jump or hop like they did, but that never deterred the Velveteen Rabbit and in the end he reaped a happy life as a real live rabbit.

The Velveteen Rabbit teaches children about giving their lives purpose and meaning and how from this purpose they will find happiness. It is a lesson we learn young, but that can become overshadowed by the demands of life when we grow into adults.

Let me share with you my own personal mission statement. This is the approach that I follow everyday in my life. It states that I will "motivate, inspire, and empower people to generate greatness through living happier and more fulfilled lives." So, do you see how my life's work, including this book, would fall under that statement?

A personal mission statement lets you know that there is more to life than just existing. It gives you purpose and knowledge that there is something that life is calling you to do. Answer that call. Don't allow your life to be filled with doubt and regret. Answer the call. You've been put on this earth to be happy. And this happiness is directly impacted by your life's purpose. So just answer the call. You life is yours to create and it starts with purpose.

Happiness as a Way of Life

But what is happiness except the simple harmony
between a man and the life he leads.

– Albert Camus

Chapter 5: Understanding the Role of Gratitude

Gratitude is a very a powerful word. When most people hear it, they associate it with a feel good emotion that comes from something good being done for them. It is so much more than that though. Gratitude is a way of life. If you embrace living a life of gratitude you will reap the benefits. Studies have shown that people who practice gratitude daily increase their personal happiness by 25%.

Not only will living a life of gratitude increase your satisfaction with life and your happiness, there are health benefits as well. This is a scientifically researched fact. Some of the best documented work comes from psychology professor, Robert Emmons. According to Dr. Emmons' research, grateful people take better care of themselves and partake in better health behaviors like regular exercise, a healthy diet, and regular physical examinations. It also shows that feeling and expressing gratitude can lower your stress rate and boost your immune system. Feeling gratitude can actually assist you in coping with daily problems, especially in managing your personal stress level.

Recent studies have shown that if you are someone who expresses gratitude during the day, you will sleep better at night. You will wake up the next day feeling more rested and energetic. With all these health benefits, a diet of gratitude may be just what the doctor ordered for you.

It is important to remember that gratitude is more than just appreciating what people do for you. It is all about being thankful for the gifts you have in your life now and expressing appreciation to others so they know what they do matters to you and that you value them. By being grateful for your life and the people around you, you will begin to notice the gratification bounces will subside and your HQC will even out, helping you more efficiently reach your "someday."

Watching a young child say their prayers at night is a humbling experience that shows true gratitude. What do they say? Kneeling there beside the bed with their eyes tightly closed and small hands clasped together, they thank God for the small things that mean the most. "Thank you God for Mommy, Daddy, my puppy Max, my friend Sam, for having Kraft Dinner for supper, for playing catch with Daddy..." Do you see that it is in the simple things in life where children find happiness? They don't ask for money or fame or success, just people they love, a friend to talk to and KD for dinner.

Surf over to Amazon.com some time and go to Children's Books and type in "Gratitude." You will be presented with pages and pages of books for children that teach them how to be grateful for the simple things in life. There is everything from *Biscuit is Thankful*, a board book for toddlers about a puppy to *The Rumpoles And the Barleys: A Little Story About Being Thankful*, a tale of mischievous mice for older readers. From the beginning, children are trained to look at the little things in life as special.

This is an easy way of finding more happiness in our lives, yet it is often overlooked by adults. Why is that? I believe that as a society, we are influenced to think negatively. Think about watching the news. It's filled with stories of tragedy, loss, financial downfalls, layoffs and more, because that's what sells. Remember, if it bleeds it leads. If you listen carefully to people around you, you'll see many choose to gravitate towards the bad things going on.

Often we struggle with seeing people with things that we perceive are bigger and better than what we have. It's a philosophy known as keeping up with the Joneses. The problem with this, is that it can lead us to take what we have in our own life for granted. We don't mean to. It's not usually an act we set out to do, but it does seem to happen. So how do we stop these feelings of negativity and turn instead to gratitude and appreciation? We must choose to do it. And we must make that choice consciously over and over again until it becomes a habit. Sound familiar? It is time to reprogram ourselves away from negative attitudes, away from envy of others and away from taking what we have for granted.

I'm not saying you shouldn't want more for your life. That's the premise of what getting to "someday" is all about. You wouldn't be reading this book if you didn't want more for yourself; more enjoyment, more happiness. I personally believe you should always be striving to be better than you are today. You should always have goals for yourself and a dream of your someday. The challenge lies in finding the balance; continuing to strive for more while appreciating what you currently have in your life. When you discover this balance, you'll be happier overall.

Places of Despair

We all face challenges in our life. It's easy to continually focus on all the things that are not going our way. This can cause us to fall into what's called a place of despair. What we tend to forget is that there are positives in even the worst situations. Admittedly, it can be hard to see them when we are faced with trying times, but there are real benefits to opening our eyes to the possibilities of good that can come from the bad. Rabbi Harold Kushner said, "If you concentrate on finding whatever is good in every situation, you will discover that your life will be suddenly filled with gratitude, a feeling that nurtures the soul."

A saying that reminds me to do this is entitled "Be Thankful." It says, "Be thankful that you don't already have everything you desire. If you did, what would there be to look forward to. Be thankful when you don't know something, for it gives you the opportunity to learn. Be thankful for the difficult times. During those times, you grow. Be thankful for your limitations because they give you opportunities for improvement. Be thankful for each new challenge because it will build your strength and character.

Be thankful for your mistakes. They will teach you valuable lessons. Be thankful when you're tired and weary because it means you've made a difference. It is easy to be thankful for the good things. A life of rich fulfillment comes to those who are also thankful for the setbacks. Gratitude can turn a negative into a positive. Find a way to be thankful for your troubles and they can become your blessings." These inspirational words can ground you when things in your life are going crazy.

Are you struggling to make it through a negative time in your life right now? Take out a piece of paper and think about other negative times in your life. How did they make you grow? What good things came out of them? Write it all down and post it up somewhere visible. We all need a reminder that good things can come out of the bad.

One of my colleagues had a child who died a few years ago. She says that the happiest day of her life and the saddest day of her life were a mere fifteen days apart. In the face of such a tragedy as this, most people would fall apart. There is an adage that says, "When you lose a parent, you lose your past; when you lose a spouse, you lose your present; when you lose a child, you lose your future." Imagine losing an entire future? Your dreams for your child?

After such heartbreak, it would be all too easy to see the negative in everything; that life was out to get you. But this wasn't the case for her. She became incredibly grateful for what she still had: a supportive family, a loving husband, friends that cared for them. And she says that she wouldn't give up those 15 days with her son for anything, despite the pain it caused in the end. She is grateful for every minute and will treasure them for the rest of her life.

She has learned how to appreciate the small things in life, like kissing her daughter goodnight. You see, one of the things she regretted most with her son was she felt she didn't tell him she loved him enough. Now, when she leaves for work in the morning or puts her daughter to bed at night, she makes sure she tells her she loves her and when she sees that sleepy smile, it fills her with happiness.

That's the power of choosing to be grateful and living in the moment.

The Gratitude Journal

Gratitude is an underrated activity. Most of us don't do nearly enough of it. Why? Much of the time it is because we don't know how to. So let's review some great ways of increasing your personal feelings of gratitude. One of the most common and effective ones is keeping a gratitude journal. At some point in your life you've probably kept a journal. You may have written down what was going on in your life on a daily basis or just kept it to record your thoughts. In a gratitude journal, you keep track of all the things you are grateful for every day.

Choose a time of day that you can sit back and write uninterrupted. I recommend right before going to bed. Use this time to reflect on what you have in your life to be grateful for. Even when you are facing a dark time, strive to find all the things you appreciate in your life. They don't need to be big things; it could be simply going for a walk with the dog or seeing the first robin of spring. Write all these down in your journal. You should try to think of at least five things each day. Focus not on possessions, but more on the blessings you have in your life. This approach helps calm and refocus your mind to live in the moment. There is something truly magical about taking a breath, looking around, and just being grateful to be alive and taking pleasure in the day.

The Alphabet Approach

If you aren't ready to commit to a journal yet, take out a piece of paper and put one letter of the alphabet on each line. As you look at each letter, think of something you're grateful for that begins with that letter. For example, for "H," you may be grateful for your health. Or under "F," perhaps you're grateful for the wonderful friends or family you have in your life. Don't take a limited approach. You can be grateful for big things in your life or very small things. Whatever you feel adds value to your life.

Once you've completed the entire alphabet, pin it up on your bulletin board or on the fridge. That way, whenever you walk by it, you will be reminded of the great things you have in your life. See the example on the next page for inspiration and ideas.

Example of the Gratitude Alphabet Exercise

What I'm Grateful For

A

B

C - Summers spent at the cottage.

D - Family dinners on Sundays.

E -

F - Great family and friends.

G - Gardening

H - My health

I -

J - Jogging in the mornings.

K - Wonderful kids

L -

M - Movie nights on Fridays

N -

O -

P - Pets

Q - Quiet time with my journal every night

R - Reading a good book.

S - Playing soccer.

T - Talking on the phone with a good friend.

U -

V - Volunteering for Relay for Life

W - Evening walks with my spouse.

X -

Y -

Z -

If you still aren't sure about the impact of gratitude, here's a great activity to try. From time to time, when my life gets a little hectic, I like to take one of those colored sticky dots that you can buy in office supply stores and put it right in the middle of the face of my watch. Therefore, every time I go to look at the time, I see this dot and it reminds me to stop, take a breath and really look at what I'm grateful for in my life.

Some people will put a special reminder in their pocket, like a small gem. This way, every time they reach in their pocket, they'll feel it and it will remind them to look around to see what they are grateful for. If you need a bigger reminder, you can actually buy "gratitude rocks" in stores or online.

These have the word "Gratitude" engraved on them and are meant to sit on your dresser or your desk. Every time you walk by them, they prompt you to remember what you have in your life to appreciate. If you can condition your mind to start to look for those things in life that you are thankful for, it will dramatically influence the way you see the world and experience each day.

Developing an Attitude of Gratitude

It is vastly important to remind yourself to appreciate both the people in your life, as well as the gifts in your life. I found a great story the other day about a young girl involved in a personal growth class at her school. As part of the class, she asked her father to list six things he believed she could do to help her become a better person. Surprised by the request, he stopped to think. Truthfully, it would have been easy for him to list six things he would like to change about his teenage daughter, but he didn't. Instead, he told her he would think about it and let her know in the morning. The next morning, the girl found six pink roses on her dresser and a card that said, "Pink is for appreciation. I can't think of six things I would like to change about you. I love you the way you are." When he arrived at home that evening, his daughter was waiting at the door with tears in her eyes and gave him a big hug and said "Thank you, Dad."

At the next Parent/Teacher meeting, his daughter's teacher told him it was the most considerate thing she'd ever heard and wished more parents took the time to appreciate their children for who they truly are inside. It was then that the man realized the power of a seemingly small gesture.

We can all relate to this. At times, we would all choose to change things about those closest to us. We could choose to go on and on about these things to them, or we could do what the father did and show his daughter that he valued and appreciated her even though there were things he would have liked to change. By showing his appreciation for her, he strengthened their relationship.

It seems like a simple choice, yet how often do you do this in day-to-day life? How easy it is to come home after a long day at work and pass your frustrations on to those around you, choosing to find what's wrong with them instead of what you love about them. You notice the muddy shoes left by the back door or the empty milk container in the fridge and get angry. Let me tell you something, be grateful that you have someone to leave the empty container in the fridge.

Usually, it is those that are closest to us that miss out on our gratitude. Cynthia Ozick said, "We often take for granted the very things that most deserve our gratitude." We remember to thank the person at the corner store, the gas attendant or waitress, but we take the ones we love most in this world for granted. You may even feel that there are times when they take you for granted as well, and it's probably true.

When I've coached people on this in the past, one of the phrases I often hear is, "Oh, they know how I feel. I don't have to say it." But are you sure? People are not mind readers. Despite the fact that they may know this most of the time, doubt can trickle in. When you're frustrated or tired, you may say or do things that cause them to wonder if you truly appreciate them or love them. You may show your appreciation in your actions, but don't underestimate the power of using words to express it as well. As William Arthur Ward once said, "Feeling gratitude and not expressing it is like wrapping a present and not giving it."

If those closest to you do something specific that you're thankful for, tell them you value it. If you are just grateful in general for having them with you, tell them that too! As with all things, the more you give, the more you get. As you take the time to tell people you appreciate them, they will, in turn, begin looking for things they appreciate in you. Remember, you can't reap what you don't sow.

You may feel slightly uncomfortable when you first begin telling your family and friends how much you appreciate them, but don't let this discourage you. Keep at it, and the more you do it, the easier it will become. If you find it awkward expressing your thanks face-to-face, don't let this stop you. Swing by the store on your way home and buy a package of thank-you notes. Sit down tonight and think about three people who have made a difference to you and you'd like to know it. Write it and send them out into the world. If you don't feel a thank you note is enough, write a letter and hand deliver it. Can you imagine the impact you will have on their day? And how will you feel afterwards? Great, I bet. There is nothing to lose by sharing your gratitude with those people in your life who deserve it.

Keep in mind, that I'm not saying that you should lavish those around you with so much praise that it begins to take on the tinge of falsehood. I'm merely reminding you that it is easy to forget to express our gratitude and we should be mindful of this and make an effort to do so sincerely. As you become more comfortable expressing gratitude to people around you, you will begin to adopt an "attitude of gratitude."

By taking the time to appreciate your accomplishments and the gifts you have in your life, you are more likely to achieve the goals you have set out for yourself. Then you will go on to set even bigger ones.

If you are not grateful, no matter how much you have, you will not be happy because you will always yearn for something more. Living a life of gratitude grounds you. It redirects your mind to find and value the positives in your life. Being grateful is the key to a happy life, a key that you hold in your hand.

Melodie Beattie said, "Gratitude unlocks the fullness of life. It turns what we have into enough and more. It turns denial into acceptance, chaos into order, confusion into clarity. It turns problems into gifts, failures into successes, the unexpected into perfect timing, and mistakes into important events. Gratitude makes sense of our past, brings peace for today, and creates a vision for tomorrow."

Chapter 6: Keeping a Positive Attitude

I remember years ago I asked my father how he was doing and he said he was great. What you'd expect, right? And then he said that every morning you wake up and stretch and you don't hit any wood, it's a pretty good day. You're on the right side of the grass. Every day may not be good, but there's good in every day.

The benefits of positive thinking and having a positive attitude are well documented. Online you will find pages of findings from researchers around the world on how people with positive attitudes are happier, healthier and live longer than those who practice habitual negative thinking.

Dr. Christopher Peterson described the benefits of a positive attitude in his book, *A Primer in Positive Psychology*. He stated that optimism is linked to positive mood and good morale, to perseverance and effective problem-solving, to academic, athletic, military, occupational, and political success, to popularity, to good health, and even to long life and freedom from trauma. Happiness is an attitude. It is a choice. We can either make ourselves miserable and weak, or we make ourselves happy and strong. The amount of work is the same in both cases.

So what is a positive attitude? A positive attitude is not about denial, nor being unrealistic. A positive attitude acknowledges the negative aspects of a situation, but

88

chooses to focus instead on the possibilities and opportunities available within that situation.

Children are naturally positive thinkers. There is nothing a child can't do, at least in their minds. We encourage this. When they feel down, we bring them back up again. Moreover, classic fairy tales breed positive attitudes in children by encouraging them to dream and by telling them they can achieve any of these dreams if they believe and work hard. It is as we grow older that doubt and uncertainties begin to weed their way into our psyche and we become skeptics.

The Power of a Button

Here's an example of the impact of a positive attitude in real life. A husband and wife run a family bakery business that has been in the family for three generations. The staff is always upbeat and happy, and the customers love visiting the bakery for both the food and the camaraderie. For as long as anyone can remember, the current owners and previous generations of owners were extremely positive and happy people. You would assume that the positive attitude was because they ran a successful business, but, in fact, it was the other way around.

The couple likes to draw attention to what is going right, so they always wear a button that states "Business is awesome." Like every other business, the family bakery has had its ups and downs over the years, but what you can always depend on is the owners' attitude and the button stating "Business is awesome."

Think about if you were to visit this bakery for the first time. As you ponder what to purchase from the plethora of sugary treats, you look up and see the button for the first time. Would you not comment on it? Probably asking, "What's so awesome about business?" This would create an uplifting conversation about the positive aspects of business, work and even life. An employee might tell you about the pleasure they get from meeting and talking to different people each day. Or the baker may tell you about the reward that comes from helping the staff grow and learn new things. His wife might say that it doesn't feel like work because she goes home in a fantastic mood from working with people she likes and doing what she enjoys all day.

I believe it was the attitude that created the button that made the business successful. By always looking for the positive, you will find it.

Your button should say: Life is awesome. By putting it out there, it will create momentum for an awesome life. You will begin to believe it. You will begin to act it. And others will begin to see and treat you that way as well.

I'm sure you know a person like this already. The kind of person whom you ask "How are you doing?" and they consistently answer with comments like, "Any better and I'd be twins." No matter what is going on, they are upbeat and positive. How does that make you feel? Do you wonder how they can always answer optimistically? Because they choose to. They choose to answer that way and choose to have a good day.

What if you actually did wear a button that said "Life is awesome"? What do you think would happen? It would certainly spark some exciting conversations for you. All day long when somebody read your button they would ask you why your life is so awesome. And you could spend time sharing the positive things in your life. If you knew you needed to give a positive answer, then wouldn't you be looking for positive things all day?

I was always taught that you wear your attitude like you wear your clothes. Others see your attitude and act accordingly. I don't need to be wearing an actual button that says "Life is awesome" or "Life stinks" for people to

figure out what my attitude is that day. Experience has taught me that the way people treat me and interact with me is directly impacted by the invisible button I have on. If I want more positivity in my life, then I need to wear my "Life is awesome" button and attract positive people and situations into my life.

One of my daily objectives is to leave every person I interact with a little more positive than when we started. Whether this is making them see the bright side of life or just shining a ray of light into a bad day. With this objective in mind, the only way I can accomplish this is to continually focus on my positive attitude. Your attitude determines what you get out of life. If you look for the good in each day, you will find it. If you look for the bad, you will find it as well. Whatever you look for is your choice.

When faced with a situation that could be perceived as bad, ask yourself this: Does having a negative attitude make the situation any better? What does it accomplish? You will find that having a negative attitude creates more stress in your life and reduces your productivity. It is much more effective and pleasant to have a positive one.

You will find that if you maintain a positive attitude, more people will want to be around you. Think of your life right now. Do you have people that call you on the phone and when you see their number on call display you don't answer it because you know they are just going to complain about everything in their life? (Are you sure you aren't one of those people?) There are people in this world who have a knack for finding what is wrong with everything in life. In order to maintain your own positive attitude, you need to minimize your contact with these people, as well as negative situations.

There are simple things you can do right now to combat a negative attitude when it strikes. First, get out and clear your head. Go for a walk when you are in a foul mood, usually just the warmth of the sun on your face will be enough to cheer you up.

Second, you need to be mindful of those around you. Negative attitudes are contagious. You may have caught your negative attitude from someone else. If this is the case, remove yourself from the situation. If you can't do so, be aware of it and make a conscious effort to not let it bring you down.

Third, insulate yourself. Turn off the news, or at the very least, don't watch it right before bed. Instead, listen to or read positive things or write in a success journal. Fill your life with positive things: blogs, books, sayings, quotes, and conferences, anything that fuels positivity in your life.

Fourth, start and end with positivity. Be sure to start your day with positive thoughts and end it the same way.

Fifth, remember that you are responsible for your attitude. You choose how you react to things around you. You cannot blame anyone else. Instead, take responsibility for it and change it.

Creating and maintaining a positive attitude is not an easy task. It is a process that requires work and commitment, however, the payoffs in your life will be huge. There will be times when you will face challenges that will threaten your ability to keep a positive attitude. It is important to prompt yourself to focus on the good that you can find. Remind yourself that you have the ability to handle what comes your way. You just need to navigate through it without letting negativity take hold. In fact, a study has shown that 95% of your emotions are determined by how you interpret events to yourself.

It does truly come down to you. You can choose not to be negative. You can choose to surround yourself with positive people and positive things. You can choose to walk away from negativity when you encounter it. You can choose to face your day with a smile. You can choose to end your day on a positive note. All this is your personal choice.

Wayne Dyer once said, "If you change the way you look at things, the things you look at change." Let me illustrate this with a story that has been passed on throughout the years about two travelers.

One day a traveler is walking along a road on a journey from one village to another. As he passed by a field, he noticed a monk tending the crops nearest to the road. The monk said, good day to the traveler who nodded in return. The traveler then turned to the monk and said, "Excuse me. Do you mind if I ask you a question?

"Not at all," replied the monk.

"I'm traveling from the village in the mountains to the village in the valley and I was wondering if you knew what it is like there?"

"Tell me," said the monk, "what was your experience at the village in the mountains?"

"Dreadful," replied the traveler. "To be honest, I'm glad to be away from there. I found the people most unwelcoming. When I first arrived, I was greeted coldly. I was never made to feel a part of the village no matter how hard I tried. The villagers kept very much to themselves. They don't take kindly to strangers. So tell me, what can I expect in the village in the valley?"

"I'm sorry to tell you," said the monk, "but I think your experience will be much the same there."

The traveler hung his head despondently and walked on.

A little while later, another traveler came upon the monk working in the field and began speaking to him.

"I'm going to the village in the valley," he said. "Do you know what it is like?"

"I do," replied the monk. "But first, tell me, where have you come from?"

"I've come from the village in the mountains," said the traveler.

"And how was that?" asked the monk.

"It was a wonderful experience. I would have stayed if I could, but I'm committed to traveling on. I felt as though I was a member of the family in the village. The elders gave me so much advice. The children laughed and joked with me. The people were kind and generous. I am sad to have left there. It will always hold special memories for me. And what of the village in the valley?" he asked again.

"I think you will find it much the same," replied the monk bidding the man good-bye.

"Good day, and thank you," the traveler said and continued his journey with a smile.

Our attitude determines the experiences that we have in life, the reflections that we get from other people, whether the situations are of joy or of sadness.

Four Keys to a Positive Attitude

Try these four keys to unlock the potential of your positive attitude.

Key Number One: Fill your mind with positives

Remember the miners in the Yukon when they used to pan for gold? Think of how they scooped up everything into their pan and then began to sift it through the little holes in the sieve. They would filter out the unwanted material to find the gold nuggets. Your mind has the same capability, but you must train it. Sifting information, deciding what you want to feed your mind is imperative to building a positive attitude. Instead of living your life on autopilot, letting in any and all thoughts, consciously feed your mind positive input. Read inspirational books, take training programs, watch shows with positive messages, listen to uplifting music or call a real positive friend and go out for a cup of coffee. While you are doing this, avoid negative situations, cynics, whiners and complainers. They plug up the holes in the bottom of your pan and slow down your ability to sift out those things that do not support your golden attitude.

You've heard me mention the impact of keeping a journal. We discussed a gratitude journal specifically earlier. Why not try a success journal as well, or combine the two, keeping track of those things you are grateful for in your day and also the positive events or successes you've had as well. After a while of looking for and writing these things down, you'll realize that most of the things that happen in your life are actually positive.

Key Number Two: Fill your mind with affirmations

To build a positive attitude, you must remind yourself of your successes, your achievements and your victories, no matter how big or small they may be. Pat yourself on the back for a job well done. Refuse to let any self-doubt enter your mind. Give yourself those positive mental pep talks: "I am a confident person. I am a positive person. I make a difference." And when you make a mistake, learn to fail forward and fail graciously. There's nothing wrong with failing provided you learn a lesson from it and that you don't keep doing the same thing. This is a habit that you have to practice. It is too easy to give into the dark side and listen to the voices of doubt. There is always somebody or something ready to attack your confidence and positive outlook. Positive affirmation is one tool you can use to protect yourself from negativity, fear and doubt.

During her trying teen years when my daughter would get down on herself about comments from other kids, I would remind her of Dolly Parton's words: "I'm not offended by all the dumb blonde jokes because I know that I'm not dumb and I also know that I'm not blonde."

Key Number Three: Look for the good in others

At one time or another as children, we were all told by our mothers that if we didn't have anything nice to say, then we shouldn't say anything at all. These are wise words that transcend generations and cultures. Our words should do no harm.

I was raised with the philosophy that we treat others as a mirror reflection of the way we see ourselves. If I'm happy with whom I am it's easy to see positives in other people. On the other hand, if I'm unhappy, frustrated or negative, then it's easy to want others to be the same way. As the phrase goes, misery loves company. Look for something you like in everyone you meet. One person might have a great smile, another a wicked sense of humor or someone else might be extremely dedicated to a worthy cause. Most everyone has something in them that makes them unique and wonderful; you just need to start looking for it.

Key Number Four: Let only positive words flow from your lips

In order to build and maintain a positive attitude, you must speak positively about everything: your family, your friends, your customers, the people you work with, your health, and your future. Go out of your way to speak optimistically about everything. You'll be amazed at the reactions you receive from others. More importantly, if you keep speaking positively, you quickly become positive. Words have the ability to build up or tear down other people and yourself. So choose to build yourself up with the power of positive words. It is not always easy when you are faced with a difficult situation. It may be easier to make a sarcastic comment, but show self-constraint in these situations. Refrain from negative comments. Only positive ones will do now.

One of my friends told me about a lesson he taught his two sons when they were young (they're both grown with families of their own now). He said he had read a story about it and was so impacted by the message that he wanted to pass it on to them.

Each summer, they go down to their cottage for a week and like to have bonfires in the night. So the first day, after they had unpacked, he told the boys there were going to collect wood for the week. They set off into the woods and soon he was handing them logs and sticks to carry. However, much to the bafflement of the boys, every once in a while, he would take a piece out of their arms and toss it back into the bush.

When they returned to the cottage, the boys sat on the dock, exhausted and sweaty, and let their feet dangle into the cool water.

"Why did you make us carry so much wood, Dad?" asked his one son.

"We'll never use it all this week," piped up his brother.

"I didn't make you carry it all. You did," said my friend.

He told the boys he had given them an attitude test. As they'd tramped through the woods, he'd listened very carefully as they chatted away. Whenever they were negative or complained – about the bugs, the work or each other – he gave them another log to carry. Conversely, if they were positive – about the fun they were going to have or by helping one another over a ditch – he threw a piece of wood away.

"How do you think you did?" he asked.

Both boys glanced sheepishly at the large pile of wood stacked beside the cottage.

"Your negative attitudes are like that pile of wood. Sometimes your comments and actions are small like sticks, while others are large like logs, but either way, the more you pile on, the heavier it weighs on you," he said.

"Think of what you say and do throughout the day," he continued. "Use positivity to cancel out your negative attitude."

Why don't you try this exercise for a week or even a day? No, you don't need to carry a stack of wood, but you should have something visible. Find a container of some sort and put it where you can see it. Get a bag of marbles or even some rocks from the driveway. The same rules apply from the story, if you demonstrate a negative attitude towards someone or something put a marble in the container. Take one out when you express a positive attitude.

Or you can try carrying a small stone in your pocket. If you think negatively, it goes in your left pocket. If you think positively, take it out and move it to your right pocket. Find out whether it stays in your left pocket or your right one for most of the day.

I'm not saying that you have to completely avoid all bad or difficult situations. That is highly improbable. It's about paying attention to your thoughts and emotions. Are you approaching the situation with the attitude of "This will never work?" Or are you coming at it with an attitude of "I can find a way to make this work?" A visible reminder is a powerful tool to help us create life changing habits.

Remember, a negative attitude clearly says you cannot achieve success, but a positive attitude shouts to the world that you can. If you've been exhibiting a negative attitude and expecting failures and difficulties, now is the time to change the way you think. It's time to get rid of negative thoughts and behavior and lead a happy life. Why not start today? If you say to yourself that you have tried and failed, it only means that you have not tried enough. Developing a positive attitude is habit-forming. You must force yourself to be positive even if you don't feel it at first in order to ingrain it in your life and make it feel normal. Trust me; it will make all the difference in your life and the lives of the people around you.

Think of the shark, Bruce in the movie *Finding Nemo* who was trying to change his way of viewing other fish. He kept saying over and over again, "I am a nice shark, not a mindless eating machine. If I am to change this image, I must first change myself. Fish are friends, not food."

Conclusion

When I was 21 years old, I was faced with a life-altering decision. It's funny how we look back at defining moments in our lives and realize now the impact they had on our lives, but at the time we have no idea.

I was working two jobs: as a produce manager at a grocery store during the day and as a fitness instructor at the local health club at night. I liked what I was doing, but I felt there was something missing. While coaching one client through his workout, he told me how impressed he was with how I related to others and asked if I was interested in changing careers to train and coach people in business and life situations full-time. You can imagine my surprise, then excitement, and of course, fear. This was a great opportunity, but I was already making good money in secure jobs. While I knew there was more out there for me to be doing, fear clouded my judgment.

I needed a sounding board, so I went where I always go, to my mother and father. I knew they would be my voice of reason. After listening to my situation and asking a few questions, my parents said just the right words. In their infinite wisdom, they asked me: "Are you happy? Do you see yourself 10 or 20 years out doing what you are doing now? You have a gift to share, but only if you decide to share it. You always have a place to come home to. You have to decide. We support you either way. But you can only change your situation if you *choose* to change your situation."

Little did they know how that small conversation would shape my philosophy of life. Little did they know how that small conversation would open up possibilities I never realized. Little did they know that small conversation would change my perspective on life and lead me to develop the confidence and passion to do what I do today. I sure hope I remembered to thank them for that "small conversation."

Happiness and joy begin with taking stock of the present. Are you grateful for what is in your life? Are you confident and passionate about what you do?

And of course, don't just dream of getting to someday, make the decision. Choose to live your someday today.

My hope for you is for this book to not remain on the pages, but live in your heart and in your actions.

In the wise words of Walt Disney:

"All your dreams can come true,
if you have the courage to pursue them."

Bibliography

Chapter 1. Getting More Enjoyment Out of Life

My Urologist. Scrubs. Prod. Touchstone Television. NBC.
    16 May 2006.

Chapter 2. Overcoming Your Fears

James, Brian. The Shark Who Was Afraid of Everything!
    New York: Scholastic, 2002.

Chapter 4. Discovering Your Life Purpose

Jerry Maguire. Writ., dir. and prod. Cameron Crowe. Prod.
    James L. Brooks, Laurence Mark Richard Sakai. Tristar
    Pictures, 1996.

Williams, Margery. The Velveteen Rabbit. New York:
    Square Fish, 2008.

Chapter 6. Keeping a Positive Attitude

Peterson, Christopher. A Primer in Positive Psychology.
    New York, Oxford University Press, 2006.

<u>Finding Nemo</u>. Writ. and dir. Andrew Stanton. Writ. Bob
    Peterson and David Reynolds. Prod. Graham Walters,
    jinko Gotoh and John Lasseter. Pixar Animation Studios,
    2003.

About the Author

Gary Gzik has been in the field of personal and professional growth for 26 years. He is an international public speaker, CEO of BizXcel Inc., a corporate trainer, a champion of Getting to Someday and an all around enthusiastic guy.

Through his presentations, training seminars, audios and books, he motivates, inspires and empowers people to generate greatness through living happier and more fulfilled lives.

Gary lives on the St. Lawrence River with his wife Jane, children Evan and Hannah and dogs, Molly and Lilly.

You can contact Gary at:

BizXcel Inc.
51 King St West Suite 201
Brockville Ontario Canada, K6V 3P8
1-866-905-2228
ggzik@bizxcel.com

www.bizxcel.com
www.gettingtosomeday.com